I Am Thankful God Gave Us

JAMES ANDERSON

INKS & BINDINGS

Inks and Bindings
888-290-5218
www.inksandbindings.com
orders@inksandbindings.com

I am thankful God
gave us the sun.

I am thankful God
gave us the moon.

I am thankful God
gave us clouds.

I am thankful God
gave us water.

I am thankful God
gave us weather.

I am thankful God
gave us rainbows.

I am thankful God gave
us beautiful flowers.

I am thankful God gave us trees.

I am thankful God gave us birds.

I am thankful God gave us butterflies.

I am thankful God gave us animals.

I am thankful God gave us bugs.

I am thankful God gave us dogs and cats.

I am thankful God gave us Jesus.

I am thankful
God
gave me

you

place child's picture here

www.ingramcontent.com/pod-product-compliance
Lightning Source LLC
Chambersburg PA
CBHW040850120626
46547CB00001B/104